Yellow Umbrella Books are published by Red Brick Learning
7825 Telegraph Road, Bloomington, Minnesota 55438
http://www.redbricklearning.com

Library of Congress Cataloging-in-Publication Data
Bauer, David
    My apple tree/by David Bauer.
    p. cm.
    Summary: "Simple text and photos present apple trees"—Provided by publisher.
    Includes index.
    ISBN-13: 978-0-7368-5974-5 (hardcover)
    ISBN-10: 0-7368-5974-8 (hardcover)
    ISBN 0-7368-1707-7 (softcover)
    1. Apples—Juvenile literature. I. Title.
SB363.B38 2006
634'.11—dc22   2005025752

Written by David Bauer
Developed by Raindrop Publishing

Editorial Director: Mary Lindeen
Editor: Jennifer VanVoorst
Photo Researcher: Wanda Winch
Conversion Assistants: Jenny Marks, Laura Manthe

Photo Credits
Cover: David Frazier/Corbis; Title Page: New York Apple Association; Page 4:
Gary Sundermeyer/Capstone Press; Page 6: Gary Sundermeyer/Capstone Press;
Page 8: Patrick Johns/Corbis; Page 10: William Allen; Page 12: Mark E. Gibson/
Corbis; Page 14: Mark E. Gibson/Corbis; Page 16: Mark E. Gibson/Corbis

1 2 3 4 5 6 11 10 09 08 07 06

My Apple Tree

by David Bauer

Yellow Umbrella Books
for early readers

My apple tree
grows leaves.

My apple tree
grows flowers.

My apple tree
grows apples.

My apple tree
grows lots of apples!

We pick apples
from my apple tree.

We eat apples
from my apple tree.

Leaves fall from my apple tree. Soon they will grow back again.

Index